THE EVOLUTION
OF AFRICA'S MAJOR NATIONS

Botswana

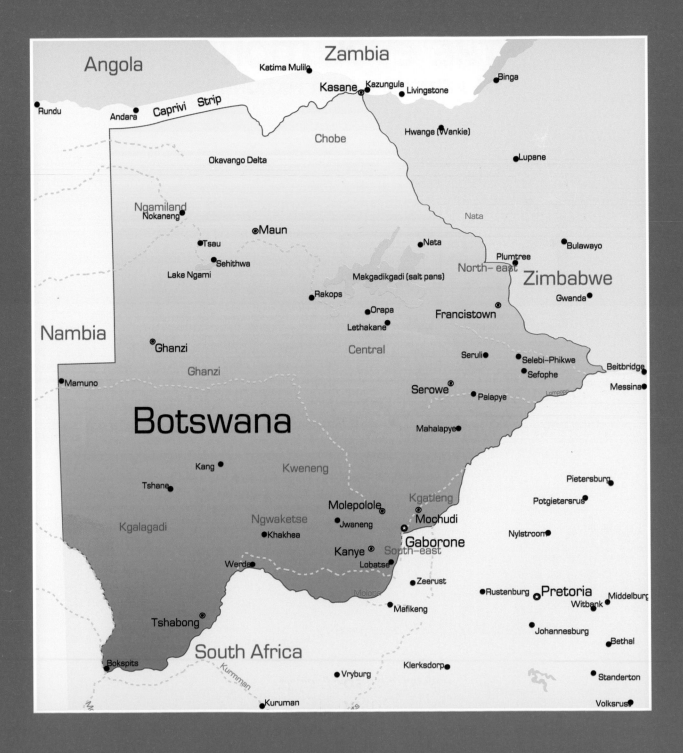

THE EVOLUTION
OF AFRICA'S MAJOR NATIONS

Botswana

Kelly Wittmann

Mason Crest
Philadelphia

Mason Crest
370 Reed Road
Broomall, PA 19008
www.masoncrest.com

CPSIA Compliance Information: Batch #EAMN2013-5. For further information,
contact Mason Crest at 1-866-MCP-Book.

First printing

1 3 5 7 9 8 6 4 2

Library of Congress Cataloging-in-Publication Data

Wittmann, Kelly.
  Botswana / Kelly Wittmann.
    p. cm. — (Evolution of Africa's major nations.)
  Includes bibliographical references and index.
  ISBN 978-1-4222-2193-8 (hardcover)
  ISBN 978-1-4222-2221-8 (pbk.)
  ISBN 978-1-4222-9433-8 (ebook)
  1. Botswana—Juvenile literature. I. Title. II. Series: Evolution of Africa's major nations.
  DT2437.W57 2012
  968.83—dc22
                              2011018530

Africa: Facts and Figures   Egypt   Nigeria

The African Union   Ethiopia   Rwanda

Algeria   Ghana   Senegal

Angola   Ivory Coast   Sierra Leone

Botswana   Kenya   South Africa

Burundi   Liberia   Sudan

Cameroon   Libya   Tanzania

Democratic Republic   Morocco   Uganda

   of the Congo   Mozambique   Zimbabwe

Table of Contents

Africa: Progress, Problems, and Promise

Robert I. Rotberg

Africa is the cradle of humankind, but for millennia it was off the familiar, beaten path of global commerce and discovery. Its many peoples therefore developed largely apart from the diffusion of modern knowledge and the spread of technological innovation until the 17th through 19th centuries. With the coming to Africa of the book, the wheel, the hoe, and the modern rifle and cannon, foreigners also brought the vastly destructive transatlantic slave trade, oppression, discrimination, and onerous colonial rule. Emerging from that crucible of European rule, Africans created nationalistic movements and then claimed their numerous national independences in the 1960s. The result is the world's largest continental assembly of new countries.

There are 53 members of the African Union, a regional political grouping, and 48 of those nations lie south of the Sahara. Fifteen of them, including mighty Ethiopia, are landlocked, making international trade and economic growth that much more arduous and expensive. Access to navigable rivers is limited, natural harbors are few, soils are poor and thin, several countries largely consist of miles and miles of sand, and tropical diseases have sapped the strength and productivity of innumerable millions. Being landlocked, having few resources (although countries along Africa's west coast have tapped into deep offshore petroleum and gas reservoirs), and being beset by malaria, tuberculosis, schistosomiasis, AIDS, and many other maladies has kept much of Africa poor for centuries.

Thirty-two of the world's poorest 44 countries are African. Hunger is common. So is rapid deforestation and desertification. Unemployment rates are often over 50 percent, for jobs are few—even in agriculture. Where Africa once was a land of small villages and a few large cities, with almost everyone engaged in growing grain or root crops or grazing cattle, camels, sheep, and goats, today more than half of all the more than 1 billion Africans, especially those who live south of the Sahara, reside in towns and cities. Traditional agriculture hardly pays, and a number of countries in Africa—particularly the smaller and more fragile ones—can no longer feed themselves.

There is not one Africa, for the continent is full of contradictions and variety. Of the 750 million people living south of the Sahara, at least 150 million live in Nigeria, 85 million in Ethiopia, 68 million in the Democratic Republic of

A cattle ranch in Botswana. Traditionally, cattle has been an important aspect of social and economic life in southern Africa. Today, the country is home to approximately 3 million cattle, and beef makes up a significant part of Botswana's agricultural exports each year.

A herd of antelopes in Chobe National Park, in northwestern Botswana. The park is home to a highly diverse selection of wildlife.

the Congo, and 49 million in South Africa. By contrast, tiny Djibouti and Equatorial Guinea have fewer than 1 million people each, and prosperous Botswana and Namibia each are under 2.2 million in population. Within some countries, even medium-sized ones like Zambia (12 million), there are a plethora of distinct ethnic groups speaking separate languages. Zambia, typical with its multitude of competing entities, has 70 such peoples, roughly broken down into four language and cultural zones. Three of those languages jostle with English for primacy.

Given the kaleidoscopic quality of African culture and deep-grained poverty, it is no wonder that Africa has developed economically and politically less rapidly than other regions. Since independence from colonial rule, weak governance has also plagued Africa and contributed significantly to the widespread poverty of its peoples. Only Botswana and offshore Mauritius have been governed democratically without interruption since independence. Both are among Africa's wealthiest countries, too, thanks to the steady application of good governance.

Aside from those two nations, and South Africa, Africa has been a continent of coups since 1960, with massive and oil-rich Nigeria suffering incessant periods of harsh, corrupt, autocratic military rule. Nearly every other country on or around the continent, small and large, has been plagued by similar bouts of instability and dictatorial rule. In the 1970s and 1980s Idi Amin ruled Uganda capriciously and Jean-Bedel Bokassa proclaimed himself emperor of the Central African Republic. Macias Nguema of Equatorial Guinea was another in that same mold. More recently Daniel arap Moi held Kenya in thrall and Robert Mugabe has imposed himself on once-prosperous Zimbabwe. In both of those cases, as in the case of Gnassingbe Eyadema in Togo and the late Mobutu Sese Seko in Congo, these presidents stole wildly and drove entire peoples and their nations into penury. Corruption is common in Africa, and so are a weak rule-of-law framework, misplaced development, high expenditures on soldiers and low expenditures on health and education, and a widespread (but not universal) refusal on the part of leaders to work well for their followers and citizens.

Conflict between groups within countries has also been common in Africa. More than 12 million Africans have been killed in civil wars since 1990, while another 9 million have become refugees. Decades of conflict in Sudan led to a January 2011 referendum in which the people of southern Sudan voted overwhelmingly to secede and form a new state. In early 2011, anti-government protests spread throughout North Africa, ultimately toppling long-standing regimes in Tunisia and Egypt. That same year, there were serious ongoing hostilities within Chad, Ivory Coast, Libya, the Niger Delta region of Nigeria, and Somalia.

Despite such dangers, despotism, and decay, Africa is improving. Botswana and Mauritius, now joined by South Africa, Senegal, Kenya, and Ghana, are beacons of democratic growth and enlightened rule. Uganda and Senegal are taking the lead in combating and reducing the spread of AIDS, and others are following. There are serious signs of the kinds of progressive economic policy changes that might lead to prosperity for more of Africa's peoples. The trajectory in Africa is positive.

Botswana is known for its picturesque landscapes. (Opposite) Beautiful sunsets are a daily occurrence in Botswana's Central Kalahari Game Reserve. (Right) Men steer their slim boats, called mokoro, through the papyrus swamps of the Okavango delta in northern Botswana. The Okavango River is one of the longest rivers in Southern Africa.

The Land

"O KAE?" THIS IS THE FRIENDLY GREETING one might hear upon arrival in Botswana. It means "How are you?" And if you're getting your first look at this marvelous country, your response will probably be a delighted "Amazed!" From the wild, pristine Chobe National Park in the north to the seemingly endless Kalahari Desert in the south, Botswana is a country of unparalleled natural beauty. And though it was sometimes overlooked in the past, in the 21st century Botswana is being recognized as the raw yet magnificent gem that it is.

Botswana is landlocked, with Angola and Zambia to its north, Zimbabwe bordering its east, South Africa to its south, and Namibia to the west. Deep in the heart of southern Africa, this gently rolling land covers approximately 220,000 square miles (569,797 square kilometers), and its elevation averages 3,300 feet (1,006 meters). It is about the size of Texas, and its terrain transitions from the thick forests of Angola to the vast deserts of South Africa. This makes Botswana one of the most geographically varied countries on the African continent.

CLIMATE

Botswana is subtropical. The temperature varies greatly depending on whether it is day or night, summer or winter. Summer runs from November through April, with temperatures averaging around 70° Fahrenheit (21° Celsius) and as high as 100°F (38°C). In winter, which is from May to October, the temperature has been known to plunge to 20°F (-7°C).

Botswana is bathed in bright sunlight for much of the year, and rainfall and humidity are low. In the north the average rainfall is about 25 inches (63.5 centimeters) per year, but in the south just nine inches (23 cm) or less is common. During the dry season, which lasts from May to August, less than 10 percent of the yearly rainfall occurs.

Botswana's climate figures prominently in one of its major industries—tourism. With many areas of Botswana sunny and pleasant for much of the year, it is a natural magnet for tourists from Europe, North America, and Asia, as well as other African countries. The government needs to encourage tourism for economic reasons, but it also wants to protect the country's delicate ecology. This can be a difficult balancing act.

A JEWEL OF NATURE

In northern Botswana there are a few areas of *miombo* woodlands. These forests grow on rock formations and contain semi-evergreen deciduous trees.

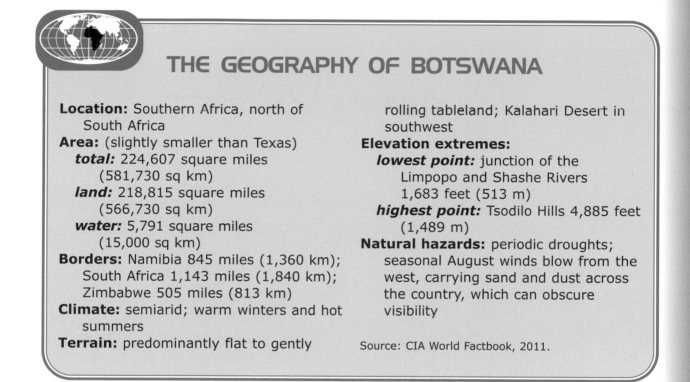

THE GEOGRAPHY OF BOTSWANA

Location: Southern Africa, north of South Africa

Area: (slightly smaller than Texas)
total: 224,607 square miles (581,730 sq km)
land: 218,815 square miles (566,730 sq km)
water: 5,791 square miles (15,000 sq km)

Borders: Namibia 845 miles (1,360 km); South Africa 1,143 miles (1,840 km); Zimbabwe 505 miles (813 km)

Climate: semiarid; warm winters and hot summers

Terrain: predominantly flat to gently rolling tableland; Kalahari Desert in southwest

Elevation extremes:
lowest point: junction of the Limpopo and Shashe Rivers 1,683 feet (513 m)
highest point: Tsodilo Hills 4,885 feet (1,489 m)

Natural hazards: periodic droughts; seasonal August winds blow from the west, carrying sand and dust across the country, which can obscure visibility

Source: CIA World Factbook, 2011.

Semi-evergreen trees are capable of keeping their leaves all year under certain conditions. In miombo forests sufficient water is the main factor in determining whether or not the trees will remain green.

In these wooded areas tall Zambezi teak trees, called *mukusi* by the people of Botswana, provide shade for other lush vegetation. Herbs and grasses thrive under these towering trees. The leaves of the trees do not interlock into a canopy, so shorter vegetation also has access to sunlight.

The wood from the teak trees is highly valued, but a good portion of the miombo woodland falls under the protection of Chobe National Park, making it inaccessible to the lumber industry. The species of trees harvested from miombo woodlands grow slowly, so resources take a long time to replenish, making logging a difficult industry to sustain. Local communities rely on the forests for building materials, fuel for cooking fires, fruit, wild game, and medicine.

Many animal species depend on the miombo woodlands as well. The forests are home to most of Africa's remaining wild dogs, which were nearly destroyed by loss of habitat, fatal interactions with humans, and disease.

A female dog and her pups stand outside the entrance to their den. It is estimated that there are fewer than 5,000 wild dogs left in Africa.

Elephants also frequent the woodlands, which provide them with large quantities of trees for food. Because the elephants tear down so many trees, some bird species, like the black-faced sandgrouse and southern ground hornbill, find their nesting places threatened. In order to protect the birds, the elephant populations must be kept below a certain level.

To the southeast and southwest of the miombo woodlands are areas of mopane woodland. The mopane tree is also known as the butterfly tree because of its leaves, which resemble butterfly wings. The mopane are able to grow quite tall in soil with a high clay content, like the soils of the Okavango-Linyanti region. Because of their height they are sometimes known as "cathedral mopane." Yet, despite their height, the mopane do not shelter the kind of vegetation one would see under the Zambezi teak.

In the northeast of Botswana are the wetlands of the Okavango Delta, which surround and overlap the Moremi game park. The Okavango River empties into the Kalahari Desert, creating an oasis that is the world's largest inland delta. There is water in this area all year so it can support many types of animals. The rare sitatunga (marshbuck) lives in the swampy areas where papyrus is abundant, while impala and topi (tsessebe) browse the delta grasslands. During the dry season huge herds of elephants, zebra, and wildebeest migrate to the Okavango Delta from the Kalahari Desert to the south.

Traveling east from the Okavango Delta one finds the Nxai Pan and the Makgadikgadi Pans. A pan is an isolated, shallow pool of water. No rivers or lakes feed into them or carry their water away. Pans form during the rainy season, and because they are not absorbed by the clay soil, they provide drinking water for many species of animals all summer long. The

Makgadikgadi Pans have very high concentrations of mineral salts, which makes them devoid of vegetation. From December to April, however, the pans fill with rainwater, and the zebra and flamingo populations spike.

The Nxai Pan is known for its baobab trees. Baobabs store water in their broad trunks, have palm-like leaves, and grow a fruit that resembles a gourd. The pulp from this fruit is called "monkey bread" by the people of the area. Baobabs have been known to live for a thousand years, and when they die, they collapse into a pile of splinters, as though they had never been.

An African legend explains the baobab tree's strange appearance. At one time, the baobab wanted to be the most beautiful tree in the world. It kept asking the creator god to give it features it admired from other trees, like height or attractive leaves. The creator grew tired of being asked to make changes, so he uprooted the baobab and shoved it back in the ground upside down.

The central and southern areas of Botswana are covered by a vast sheet of sand. This is the great Kalahari Desert, which extends west into Namibia and south into South Africa. Although the Kalahari is called a desert, it contains more than just sand dunes and rock formations. Some parts of the Kalahari receive occasional rainfall, and as a result these areas contain trees, shrubs, and grasses. The most common tree in the Kalahari is the silver terminalia. Sometimes, when stunted, these trees look more like bushes—low to the ground with distinctive flattened canopies. Under the trees of the Kalahari grow bushes and shrubs, along with a silky grass called "bushman's grass."

A PLACE TO ROAM FREE

There are fewer species of big game in the Kalahari Desert than there are in the moister wetland and woodland areas simply because there are fewer watering holes. Big game animals require a lot of food, which depends on water. However, there are still many fascinating animals to see, including perhaps the most populous creature in the Kalahari: springbok. Springbok are small brown and white gazelles known for the graceful way they leap across the desert. Like most prey animals, springbok are herbivores, meaning they subsist on plants. Gemsbok are another common antelope found in the desert. They look similar to the East African oryx; sometimes the oryx is considered a subspecies of gemsbok. Gemsbok do not have to drink from a watering hole in order to meet their water needs, making them an ideal desert animal. Male gemsbok have long, straight horns that angle back from their heads. In addition to these antelope, there is also the eland, one of the largest antelope species. Elands can weigh anywhere from 800 pounds (363 kilograms) to over 2,000 pounds (907 kg).

Preying on these herbivores are the carnivores, or meat-eaters, including lions, leopards, cheetahs, and spotted hyenas. The lion prides of the Kalahari Desert are particularly interesting because they are different from their counterparts in the savannah. Kalahari lion prides roam over great distances and are loosely bound. Members of prides live alone or in pairs and can go for years without seeing close family members. The lions are leaner than those found elsewhere, and the males all have scruffy black manes. Kalahari lions are also able to survive on less water than lions in other areas. Smaller carnivores in the desert include the black-backed jackal, the honey badger, and the aardwolf.

Botswana is also home to a wide variety of bird species, and very few of the 550 species that live in the country are seriously threatened by predators. During the rainy season the land is full of fruits and insects, which gives the birds plenty to eat. The most noticeable avian in Botswana is probably the ostrich, which is the world's largest bird. The ostrich is a resident bird species, meaning it lives in the area all year round. Also found in Botswana is the unique openbill stork. This bird has a large bill which does not close except at the very tip. Their peculiar bills are used to extract snails from their shells. The upper section holds the shell down while the sharp, lower bill cuts the snail out. Many of the birds species found in Botswana are *migrants* that fly in, usually from Europe, and stay from September until May.

TRANSFRONTIER CONSERVATION

Some animal species in Botswana, such as the wildebeest, have seen their numbers dwindle recently because of the fences erected to protect farmers'

A herd of springbok in the Kalahari Gemsbok National Park. For unknown reasons, springbok will sometimes "pronk," leaping high into the air with their backs arched. It is thought that this may tell predators that they have been spotted.

herds from diseases carried by wild animals. Cattle herds are a major economic resource for the country, so there is considerable pressure to put their welfare ahead of wild animals. Fences have been built along the border with Namibia's West Caprivi Game Reserve, as well as through the wilderness of Ngamiland and northern Botswana. The fences keep the wild game from migrating to water, and many die while trying to find a way around them. The country is currently looking for ways to solve this problem.

To protect its national parks the Botswanan government has ordered regular patrols to discourage poachers. Through a combination of anti-poaching tactics and successful land management, Botswana has created an environment in which game thrive. Currently, there are so many elephants in the country that the government has requested that they be removed from the endangered species list. There are so many, in fact, that they are threatening crops both in Botswana and in neighboring Namibia.

Since wildlife knows no borders and big game animals tend to move over large areas of land, leaders in Botswana have to work with the leaders

Wildebeest on the move in Okavango National Park.

of other African countries to save threatened species. This is called ***transfrontier conservation***, an idea that has many proponents in the conservation community, including Pete Le Roux, general manager of the Mashatu Game Reserve. Le Roux has devoted his life to saving the wildlife of southern Africa, and he believes that tourism is the best hope for the survival of many endangered species. In an interview with *National Geographic*, Mashatu's business manager David Evans explained, "The only way conservation can work is if it is self-sustainable. At some stage it's got to pay its own way." Le Roux, Evans, and other animal advocates are pleased to see the governments of Botswana, South Africa, and Zimbabwe working together to maintain transfrontier game parks and encourage tourism.

People have lived in the Botswana area for many thousands of years. (Opposite) This cave painting in the Tsodilo Hills depicts an antelope. (Right) A Tswana woman carries a baby on her back and firewood on her head. The Tswana inhabited South Africa before migrating west in the 19th century.

2 The Long Journey to Independence

THE REGION THAT TODAY is known as Botswana has been inhabited for thousands of years. Cave paintings found in the Tsodilo Hills of the Kalahari Desert—which archeologists believe may be 26,000 years old—depict humans hunting, fishing, gathering food, and celebrating. Archeologists have also found human skeletons believed to be 15,000 years old, which may be ancestors of the Khoesan people. The Khoesan were hunter-gatherers who used wood, stone, and animal bones to make tools and weapons. Around 2,200 years ago the Khoesan split into the Khoe and San tribes. The Khoe adopted cattle and goat herding practices, while the San remained hunter-gatherers.

By the fourth century A.D. Bantu tribes from the north had migrated south. Their knowledge of farming and iron smelting spread to neighboring tribes. With this knowledge the people in Botswana began to settle into permanent communities, plant fields of crops, dig wells to sustain themselves during dry seasons, and make more advanced weapons. While no written history of Botswana exists before the 18th century, modern scholars have learned about the cultures of the region from traditional stories and songs handed down through the generations.

THE ARRIVAL OF THE TSWANA

The people who would give their name to the country of Botswana came to the area in the early 19th century, migrating north from what is now South Africa. They are known as the Tswana and are now the major ethnic group in Botswana. (The term Batswana is now used to describe all the citizens of Botswana, whether they actually descend from the Tswana or not.) The Tswana had an ordered society in which people were organized under ward chiefs, with one king reigning supreme.

The main reason the Tswana moved north was to escape a period of unrest known as *Mfecane* (the scattering), during which tribes such as the Zulu, Lesotho, and Ngwane (or Swazi) fought for control of territory and sources of water in the southern tip of Africa. The Tswana migration was a peaceful one. There is no evidence of territorial disputes between the Tswana and the people already inhabiting modern-day Botswana.

Once the Tswana arrived in their new home, they changed their way of living. Rather than settling in small villages in open country, as had been their custom, the Tswana began to build larger towns on hills. These towns would be stronger and easier to defend from enemies. Their buildings became stronger and more permanent, often with walls of stone rather than grass matting.

With greater security came a period of abundance and wealth. The Tswana states of Ngwato, Kwena, and Ngwaketse engaged in friendly economic competition. They traded ivory, ostrich feathers, and other commodities to Europeans (primarily Portuguese from the west coast of Africa or Dutch and English colonists from southern Africa) for weapons, clothing, and jewelry. In the mid-19th century the Tswana reached the height of their power, and their cities were relatively safe and secure.

TRADERS, EXPLORERS, AND MISSIONARIES

For Europeans during the 19th century, traveling in Botswana was a challenge. The white traders used horses and oxen to pull their wooden wagons through the vast and dangerous land at a pace of about 12 miles (20 km) per day. *Hydration* was a constant concern. Not only was it almost impossible to carry an adequate quantity of water, but the quality of the water was often so bad that it killed both the men and the animals. Another danger was disease carried by the flies and ticks that tortured the trading parties as they made their way through the wilderness.

These traders introduced the concept of paper money to the people of Botswana. Before the Europeans all products had been traded in a *barter system*. Money is not used in a barter system. Instead, possessions (such as livestock), products (like wool, leather, or meat), or other goods are traded for goods or services, as negotiated by the two people involved in the trade.

A missionary preaches the Christian gospel to a gathering of African children. In addition to their religious message, missionaries often introduced new technologies or medicines to the people of Africa.

Some of the Europeans who came to Botswana had loftier goals than just trading, though. They were explorers and missionaries who wanted to expose the Batswana to European ways of thinking and living, thereby "civilizing" them. They were not concerned that the Batswana had their own civilization, or that most of them were quite happy living without Western culture or religion.

Many of the things the missionaries did were very controversial, even at the time. They did all they could to destroy the native culture of the Batswana and were not interested in understanding or appreciating the many beautiful aspects of African culture. Yet some things they did helped the people of this region in practical ways. Missionaries taught African farmers how to maximize their time and strength by using plows and wagons and how to more effectively irrigate their crops. Missionary women set up hospitals where they cared for the sick and delivered babies, and Europeans of both sexes were involved in founding schools for the Batswana's children.

UNDER BRITISH PROTECTION

Beginning in the 1850s the Batswana found themselves increasingly threatened by the Boers, European farmers who occupied areas in southeastern Africa. The Boers were descended from Dutch, German, Flemish, and Scandinavian immigrants and were semi-nomadic. A fear that the Boers might move north made the Batswana worried about their own security. They did not want to lose their land, so tribal leaders turned to the British government for help, asking for protection.

When the British finally decided to lend a hand, it was for their own purposes, not out of any great love for the Batswana. The British were worried about the "north road" that led into the heart of Africa. They feared that the Boers might join with the German government, which controlled colonies in

Central Africa, and restrict English access to this vital trade route. The loss of this road would be a disaster for British trade in Africa, so in 1885 Botswana became a *protectorate* of Britain called Bechuanaland.

For the next 70 years black Africans in Botswana lived under the rule of the British crown. Eventually, a goal of the British became to bring Botswana into the Union of South Africa, which was formed in 1910 after the British defeated the Boers in the Anglo-Boer War (1899–1902). Seeing how black Africans were treated in South Africa, however, the Batswana fought against being absorbed into the Union. Whites ruled the Union of South Africa, and blacks were denied basic human rights, so the Batswana were determined to remain separate.

THE ROAD TO DEMOCRACY

Seretse Khama was the heir to a dynasty that had held traditional tribal rule in Botswana for over a century. After graduating from Fort Hare University College in South Africa, he moved to England to attend Oxford University. In 1947 he married an English woman, Ruth Williams. Because of his time in England, Khama had the advantage of being able to understand both African and British cultures. When his education was complete, Khama and his wife moved to Botswana and immediately began to work for the democratic cause. Their interracial marriage caused an uproar in South Africa, where *apartheid* had made racial mixing illegal. The apartheid government did not want its northern neighbor affecting the opinions of its people. The British were pressured to depose Khama and eventually exiled him in 1951 for fear of losing South African gold and uranium. In response, Botswanans rioted.

In 1956 Britain buckled to worldwide criticism and allowed Khama to return to Botswana. Khama continued working for the country's independence, and in 1961 he joined the British legislative council. The purpose of this advisory governmental body was to bring Botswana closer to independence. The council received criticism from political parties such as the Botswana Independence Party and the Botswana People's Party. These parties supported radical measures, such as the nationalization of some lands and businesses and the removal of white people from the government, and were not interested in the more conservative goals of the legislative council. Khama disagreed strongly with the agenda of these groups. He wanted to work with whites for a peaceful, nonviolent transition to democracy.

This photo of Seretse Khama and his wife Ruth was taken in 1964, a year before Khama became prime minister of Bechuanaland. Khama's policies as president of Botswana helped make the country one of Africa's most stable democracies.

Khama knew he was in for an uphill battle. His countrymen were fed up and wanted change to come as quickly as possible. So in 1961 in Gaborone

(which would soon become his nation's new capital) he and five other edu-
cated, politically skilled Batswana leaders formed the Botswana Democratic
Party (BDP). The goal of this party was to bring freedom and civil rights to
the blacks of Botswana without violence and bloodshed. The leaders of the
BDP traveled the country speaking to as many people as they could. They
convinced many that a radical government would only cause trouble, both
domestically and internationally, and that a better solution was to work with
the British government to ensure a smooth transition to independence.

**Supporters of Festus Mogae, leader of the Bostwana Democratic Party,
celebrate at a rally before election day in October 2004. The Botswana
Democratic Party won 44 out of 57 seats in that legislative election.**

The tactics Khama and his cohorts used succeeded, and events moved quickly. In 1964 Britain accepted proposals for self-government in Botswana. In 1965 a constitution was written, and in 1966 Botswana became an independent country. Seretse Khama, who had worked so long and hard for this peaceful transfer of power, was elected Botswana's first president. He was subsequently reelected twice and served in that position until his death in 1980.

Since gaining its independence, Botswana has been a rare example of democracy on a continent that is often torn by authoritarian governments, war, and racial tension. Its people have high hopes that their peaceful way of life will continue.

The city of Gaborone is the capital of Botswana and home to most government offices. (Opposite) The 57 members of Botswana's National Assembly meet in this building. (Right) Gaborone residents wait in line in order to cast their vote in a presidential election.

3 Democracy in Action

THE CONSTITUTION OF 1966 called for a separation of powers much like that of the United States. The three branches of government are the executive branch, the legislative branch, and the judicial branch. The executive branch is headed by the president, who serves as the head of government and the symbolic face of Botswana to the world. The legislative branch is made of the National Assembly, with a House of Chiefs in consultation. The judicial branch consists of the High Court, a Court of Appeal, and a Magistrate's Court for each district. Unlike in the United States, however, the president of Botswana is not chosen by a general election but by whichever party holds a majority in the National Assembly.

Local governments have a lot of power in Botswana, and their organization can vary greatly. The country is divided into nine districts and five towns, each with their own governing council. Some of the districts are headed by elected officials, while others have more a traditional leadership based on tribal chiefs. The central government allows these local governments to collect their own taxes and also subsidizes them with federal government grants.

The voting age in Botswana is 18, and voters from every district and town elect representatives to serve in the National Assembly. There are currently 57 elected members of the National Assembly. From these elected members the president chooses his cabinet, or closest advisors.

The House of Chiefs is an advisory group made up of 15 tribal chiefs. Its members lend their wisdom to the National Assembly and preside over customary tribal courts. Customary courts deal with minor offenses and have the ability to deal out corporal punishments, such as flogging.

Any person who does not want his or her case to be heard in traditional court can request that it be moved to the formal court system, which is based on the British legal system. The president appoints all judges to the formal court system, and these judges serve until voluntary retirement, death, or, in a few cases, removal for corruption. Removal is rare, however.

STRONG LEADERSHIP

After the death of Seretse Khama, the presidency of Botswana passed to his vice president, Ketumile Joni Masire. Masire spent most of the 1980s walking a political tightrope. Though he accepted aid from the Soviet Union, he rejected what he saw as radical communism on the continent. He did not want Botswana to become a communist state, which would have brought it into the *Cold War*.

When the African National Congress (ANC), a political party in South Africa, appealed to Botswana to shelter its *guerrilla fighters*, it met with curt rejection. The African National Congress fought the South African government for an end to apartheid, a system in which whites and blacks were separated. When the ANC's non-violent resistance methods failed, the party began sabotaging government resources. Though Botswana publicly decried South Africa's system of apartheid, it was too economically dependent on its southern neighbor to support those fighting against the government. Helping the ANC would have meant losing a vital trade partner. Despite Botswana's official ban on ANC activities within its borders, the ANC established bases in Botswana that were eventually attacked by the South African Defense Forces. Finally, in the early 1990s, South Africa took steps towards ending apartheid and giving equal civil rights to blacks. The African National Congress came out of exile and ceased its attacks against the South African government, which led to more peaceful relations with Botswana.

Sir Ketumile Masire of Botswana addresses the United Nations. In 1998 he retired after 18 years as president and was replaced by his vice president, Festus Mogae.

In the early 1990s the Botswana Democratic Party (BDP), still led by President Masire, continued to receive strong support in the rural areas of the country, while the Marxist-leaning Botswana National Front (BNF) made significant urban gains in the election in 1994. In that election the BNF gained 13 seats. The election was fair and peaceful, with a turnout of 70 percent, and many people in Botswana seemed to feel that these two parties kept each other in line, with neither getting too much power.

Festus Mogae was the third person to hold the office of president. During his 10 years in office, he focused on developing Botswana's economy.

The next president of Botswana, former vice-president, Festus Mogae, was inaugurated when Masire retired in 1998. Mogae was elected in his own right in 1999 and again in 2004.

In April of 2008, Mogae stepped down and was replaced by Vice President Ian Khama for an interim term. The BDP retained majority control of the National Assembly in the 2009 general elections, and Khama (the son of former president Seretse Khama) was then officially sworn in as the fourth president of Botswana.

The Batswana's desire for peace and security shows in the smooth transitions of the presidency since the late 1960s, and the fact that there have been only four presidents, all from the same party. However, while President Mogae was seen as a stable, conservative figure who made no major changes in the way the country was governed, President Khama has proved to be a little more controversial. Two of his most unpopular legislative changes include a high tax on alcoholic beverages and the creation of the Media Practitioners Law, which allows the government to decide what is and what is not good journalism. Critics argue that this limits the people's right to free speech and freedom of the press. Furthermore, Khama's creation of the Directorate of Internal Security (DIS) has been viewed by some as a move towards more authoritarian control. The DIS is a police agency, designed to function like the FBI in the U.S., but several recent killings linked to the DIS suggest the agency might be operating outside the rule of law.

Despite these internal controversies, Khama has shown a clear support for democracy in his foreign policy. He was among the first African leaders to speak out against

Ian Khama has served as the president of Botswana since April 2008.

Robert Mugabe's anti-democratic actions in neighboring Zimbabwe, and has also criticized Sudan's president, Omar al-Bashir, for failing to stop the genocide in Darfur. Both actions have earned him a lot of respect worldwide.

Botswana's economy is one of the strongest in Africa. (Opposite) Blasted kimberlite containing diamonds is loaded onto a truck for transport. (Right) Tourism is a major industry in Botswana. Foreign visitors spend more than $1 billion each year in the country.

4 Botswana's Impressive Economy

BECAUSE OF ITS COPIOUS NATURAL RESOURCES and political stability, Botswana has become one of Africa's most economically successful countries. Those who argue that independence for African countries leads to economic ruin need only look to Botswana to be proven wrong: In the first 30 years after Botswana gained independence, its economic growth rate averaged about 9 percent. That made it not only one of the fastest-growing economies in Africa but in the entire world. The Gross National Income per person in 2010 was $12,840, placing it among the three most prosperous African nations. Still, recent years have not been nearly as prosperous, and many of the Batswana have yet to share in this success.

In addition, a serious health crisis has a major impact on the econom-

THE ECONOMY OF BOTSWANA

Gross domestic product (GDP*):
$28.49 billion
Inflation: 7.5% (2007 est.)
Natural resources: diamonds, copper, nickel, salt, soda ash, potash, coal, iron ore, silver
Agriculture (2.3% of GDP): livestock, sorghum, maize, millet, beans, sunflowers, groundnuts
Industry (45.8% of GDP): diamonds, copper, nickel, salt, soda ash, potash, coal, iron ore, silver; livestock processing; textiles
Services (51.9% of GDP): government, banking, tourism, other
Economic growth rate: 8.6%

Foreign trade:
Exports–$4.42 billion: diamonds, copper, nickel, soda ash, meat, textiles
Imports–$4.52 billion: foodstuffs, machinery, electrical goods, transport equipment, textiles, fuel and petroleum products, wood and paper products, metal and metal products
Currency exchange rate: U.S. $1 = 6.53 pulas (2011)

*GDP is the total value of goods and services produced in a country annually.
All figures are 2010 estimates unless otherwise indicated.
Sources: CIA World Factbook, 2011

ic growth of Botswana. In 2007, world health authorities estimated that nearly 1 in 4 Batswana between the ages of 15 and 49 had contracted HIV, ranking it second in the world for highest percentage of the population. This has left many adults too ill to work or take care of their families. Thankfully, this situation is slowly improving as new drug treatments become available. The Botswana Ministry of Health has instituted a program called MASA, meaning "new dawn." The program now distributes medicine to more than 100,000 adults and children infected with HIV, the virus that causes

AIDS. The drug treatment programs prevent the worst symptoms of the disease, enabling these people to live normal lives.

AGRICULTURE

Raising cattle has always been an important part of the lives of the Batswana. Despite the growth of the diamond industry, most of Botswana's workforce is still employed in agriculture, though it only makes up 2.3 percent of the country's *gross domestic product (GDP)*. There are almost 3 million head of cattle in Botswana. Not only do these cattle feed the Batswana, they also provide jobs for them in meat processing, hide tanning, and the manufacture of leather products. Some of these goods are sold in Botswana, while others are exported to other countries.

Sales of beef to Europe account for 90 percent of agricultural exports. The state has a *monopoly* on beef exports, and the state-run Botswana Meat Commission (BMC) coordinates production.

Foot and mouth disease, a serious cattle illness, hurt the industry after an outbreak in 2002. Thousands of cattle had to be destroyed in an attempt to eradicate the disease, and this led to many Batswana losing their jobs. The outbreak cost the BMC an estimated $4.5 million. In 2003 another $2 million was lost when a meat processing plant had to be closed so the European Union could inspect and approve the facility.

INDUSTRY

Diamonds are Botswana's most important natural resource, and diamond mining is its most profitable industry by far. Diamond mining in Botswana began in 1971 and since that time has grown steadily to the point that it now makes up one-third of the country's GDP. Botswana is now at the very top of the diamond business, producing more gem-quality diamonds than any other country in the world.

All diamond production is done by Debswana, a joint venture between the government of Botswana and the South African company DeBeers. DeBeers runs the four diamond mines in Botswana and splits the profits with the government.

Although the industry is very profitable, it is not without problems. In late 2004 Debswana's workers walked off their jobs in a *wildcat strike*. Although already the highest-paid workers in the country, with benefits such as free housing and free medical insurance, they demanded a salary raise of 16 percent. Debswana responded by firing hundreds of workers. After tense negotiations the union accepted the company's offer of a 10 percent raise.

Another fight with the diamond industry is going on in the Central Kalahari Game Reserve. In 2002 the government of Botswana prohibited the San, who traditionally live in the Kalahari, from living in the reserve. Since then, nearly all of the San have been moved to resettlement camps. The bushmen complain they have been forced to move because the government wants the land for diamond mining. The government denies that the relocation is related to mining and says that it is meant to improve the lives of the San, as resettlement areas are provided with modern facilities, such as schools and hospitals. The dispute is ongoing.

Neither of the above, however, was as problematic as the recent world-

A member of the San tribe protests outside a diamond store in London. The San believe they were evicted from the Central Kalahari Game Reserve so that land could be mined for diamonds.

wide recession and the resultant drop in diamond prices. In a drastic move to limit the global supply, Debswana decided in 2009 to cut production nearly in half, from 33 million *carats* to approximately 18 million. The move seems to have worked, as demand increased greatly in 2010 and Debswana responded by ramping up production 36 percent. After a few years of negative growth, Botswana's economy is now showing signs of recovery.

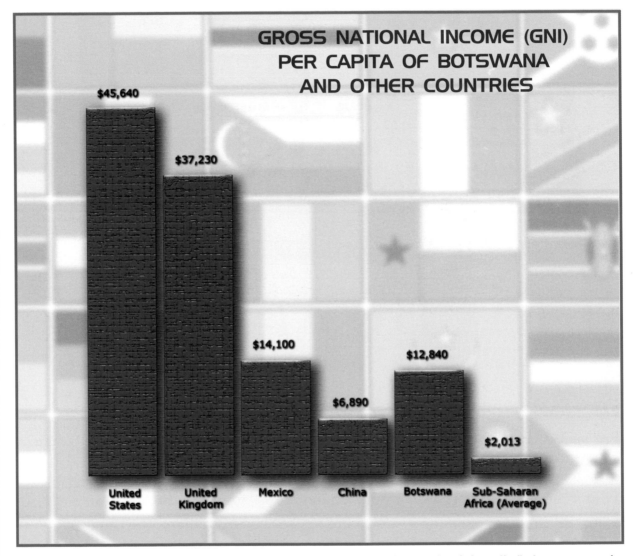

GROSS NATIONAL INCOME (GNI) PER CAPITA OF BOTSWANA AND OTHER COUNTRIES

- United States — $45,640
- United Kingdom — $37,230
- Mexico — $14,100
- China — $6,890
- Botswana — $12,840
- Sub-Saharan Africa (Average) — $2,013

Gross national income per capita is the total value of all goods and services produced domestically in a year, supplemented by income received from abroad, divided by midyear population. The above figures take into account fluctuations in currency exchange rates and differences in inflation rates across global economies, so that an international dollar has the same purchasing power as a U.S. dollar has in the United States. Source: World Bank, 2011.

The leaders of Botswana know their country cannot depend on diamonds alone if they want the economy to continue to grow. The government is responding by trying to diversify Botswana's mineral output, concentrating on developing the salt, copper, nickel, coal, iron ore, and silver industries.

SERVICES

The service sector is a very important part of Botswana's economy, accounting for 52 percent of its GDP. Tourism makes up 12 percent of that. The biggest attraction for tourists is Botswana's beautiful natural landscape, especially the big game animals that can be seen in its pristine game parks and the Okavango delta region. Many people in Botswana speak English and social strife is rare, so it is a popular destination with Westerners who might not be comfortable going into other African countries. Traveling throughout the country is also fairly easy due to the relatively good condition of its roads.

Because tourism is so important, the government works to strike a balance between what is good for the land and what is good for the economy. Excessive tourism could destroy Botswana's environment and the traditional way of life enjoyed by its rural people. This is why the government encourages *ecotourism*, in which smaller groups of tourists are taken through the wilderness or rural areas with as little damage done to the land as possible.

FOREIGN INVESTMENT

Botswana abolished its foreign exchange controls in 1999, allowing its currency to be bought and sold on the free market. And many businesses that

Two tourists take a boat ride in a traditional dugout canoe on the Chobe River. Small tour groups and personalized trips lower the ecological impact of tourism.

were once run by the government are being sold into the private sector. Along with Botswana's relative political stability and lower business taxes, these moves toward privatization make Botswana a good bet for foreign investors. Liberal economic policies like these give businesses the chance to make money unhindered by government interference. However, some regulations exist to protect businesses from being taken over by large foreign corporations. Foreign ownership may not exceed 55 percent in any publicly traded company, and no foreign individual may own more than 10 percent of a Botswanan company.

Botswana is particularly looking forward to a fruitful economic partnership with China. China has already built hospitals, schools, and roads in Botswana, and it allows its people to travel there as tourists. President Khama and other leaders are excited about the huge potential for Chinese tourism. However, there has been some friction between Chinese business people and the Batswana, as a growing influx of Chinese merchants has begun to threaten the livelihoods of local businesses. In 2009, government officials moved to ban Chinese clothes sellers, for example, who were selling knock-off brands at cut-rate prices. The government is hoping to smooth over this culture gap with a new system of merchant licensing, and reap the benefits of a long-term economic relationship with China.

(Opposite) A San father teaches his son how to hunt with a bow and arrow. The San were the original inhabitants of the Botswana area. (Right) A Botswanan man walks among newly dug graves. The high rate of AIDS infection in Botswana translates into one of the highest death rates in the world, which negatively affects the economy.

5 The People of Botswana

MOST BATSWANA SPEAK either the official language, English, or the national language, Setswana, so communication is not usually a problem. However, at least 26 different languages are spoken in Botswana, reflecting the many ethnic groups that have contributed to this country's vibrant culture.

THE SAN

The most famous of Botswana's ethnic groups is the San, or bushmen, of the Kalahari. Many linguists believe that the ancestors of the San were the first humans to develop a language. This belief has come from studying the San's distinctive clicking, clucking, and popping language, which is one of the most sophisticated and complex in the world. Within this language are many *dialects*, and tribes identify themselves based on the dialect they speak. Since

THE PEOPLE OF BOTSWANA

Population: 2,065,398 (July 2011)*
  *note: estimates for this country explicitly take into account the effects of excess mortality due to AIDS; this can result in lower life expectancy, higher infant mortality and death rates, lower population and growth rates, and changes in the distribution of population by age and sex than would otherwise be expected

Ethnic groups: Tswana 79%, Bakalanga 11%, Basarwa 3%, Other 7%

Age structure:
  0–14 years: 33.9%
  15–64 years: 62.2%
  65 years and over: 3.9%

Birth rate: 22.31 births/1,000 population

Infant mortality rate: 11.14 deaths/1,000 live births

Death rate: 10.57 deaths/1,000 population

Population growth rate: 1.66%

Life expectancy at birth:
  total population: 58.05 years
  male: 58.78 years
  female: 57.3 years

Total fertility rate: 2.5 children born/woman

Religions: Christian 71.6%, Badimo 6%, other 1.4%, unspecified 0.4%, none 20.6% (2001 census)

Languages: Setswana 78.2%, Kalanga 7.9%, Sekgalagadi 2.8%, English (official) 2.1%, other 8.6%, unspecified 0.4% (2001 census)

Literacy: 81.2% (2003 est.)

All figures are 2011 estimates unless otherwise indicated.
Source: Adapted from CIA World Factbook, 2011.

San live in small family groups there have even been times when certain dialects were developed and used only by a dozen or so people and were lost when the last member of the family died.

In San society men do all the hunting, providing about 20 percent of the food. The women, with the help of their children, concentrate on gathering wild plants, which provide the other 80 percent of the San diet. Beyond food, water collection is the other major concern for the San. They have become experts at finding water in the desert by squeezing liquid from plants and roots.

For the last decade, the San have been embroiled in a fight with Botswana's government over their forced relocation. The government has deemed that the Central Kalahari Game Reserve is meant for animals only and therefore they have moved the San to a new area. In 2006, the San won a landmark lawsuit, and Botswana's high court granted them the right to return to their ancestral homeland. So far, however, the government has hindered the process by blocking the San's access to water and trying to argue that the verdict only applies to the 189 individuals specified in the lawsuit, not the San people as a whole.

OTHER ETHNIC GROUPS

The Tswana are the largest ethnic group in Botswana, and their name is used to describe all the people who live in the country. They speak the Setswana language, which is the national language (English is the official language). Many Tswana now live in the cities, but some prefer a traditional rural life in a village, where they live in thatched mud huts. A typical Tswana villager often has three homes: one in his village, one adjacent to his farmland, and one where he keeps his cattle.

The Khoe descend from the same ethnic group as the San, but unlike the San, they own herds of cattle. They must continue to hunt and gather, however, because they do not kill their cattle for meat. Instead, their diet is milk-based. The number of cattle owned by a man indicates his social sta-

A Tswana herdsman drives his cattle across the Thamalakane River.

tus within the community, so killing the animals for food would affect his wealth and standing. The Khoe have created a complex legal code to regulate ownership and inheritance of cattle, making their lives more structured than those of the San.

The Basubiya, Hambukushu, and Bayei tribes have communities that are concentrated on rivers such as the Chobe, the Okavango, and the Linyanti. These tribes have a fish-based diet, and they are highly skilled craftsmen who make dugout canoes, harpoons, and nets to use for fishing. They also occasionally hunt big game, such as hippopotami. Hippo hunting is very dangerous, but when successful, it can provide meat for a large group of people.

The Bakalanga are the second-largest population group after the Tswana. They are *agriculturalists*, which means most of their food comes from planted crops rather than gathered wild plants. Other groups are the Ovaherero and the Ovambanderu, who live off their large herds of goats, sheep, and cattle. These animals are central to the tribes' strong religious beliefs. The Ovaherero and the Ovambanderu are easily distinguished from other Batswana because of the women's old-fashioned dress, which includes a distinctive hat.

There are far fewer white people in Botswana than in the other countries in southern Africa, and many of the white people who live there are not citizens. They are *expatriates* who come to work for a few years, then go back home to other African countries or Europe. Those white people who are citizens are usually wealthy and can trace their ancestry back to the time when Britain ruled Botswana.

RELIGION IN BOTSWANA

A little over 70 percent of all Batswana practice Christianity, the official religion of Botswana. Christian services are held in English, Setswana, and other languages. There are Anglicans, Methodists, Lutherans, Catholics, and followers of the Zion Christian Church in Botswana.

Despite people's conversions to Western faiths, traditional beliefs still play a large role in everyday life. Traditional religious practices include ancestor veneration, in which people pray to the spirits of their ancestors, ask for their help and offer them gifts to keep them happy. There is also the belief that the natural world is filled with spirits, and Africans may pray to or ask favors of the spirits of animals, plants, the soil, the sun, and the moon. Often the skills of traditional healers are used along with Western medicine to treat the sick.

Almost all Batswana take birth, wedding, and burial rites very seriously. These life passages are considered to be spiritual experiences. Other traditional rites, such as the adolescent initiation rites of *bogwera* (for men) and *bojale* (for women), have garnered disapproval from the government and fallen out of favor. *Gofethla pula*, the rain-making rite, is now practiced mainly by elderly citizens who refuse to give up the old ways.

FAMILY LIFE

It is estimated that 50 to 60 percent of households in Botswana are headed by women. This is primarily because so many men are off working in the diamond mines and other industries. For those families who live off the land, income is often seasonal or erratic, so the steady income of a mining job attracts many workers. Studies have shown that poverty is higher among female-headed households in the cities, but in rural areas, the income of female-headed households is about the same as in households headed by men.

Though one-third of Botswana's families live below the international poverty line, 95 percent of the population has access to safe water. Ninety-six percent of children under the age of one have also been immunized against diseases like diphtheria and polio. The birth rate is low for an African country, which enables families to better care for the children they do have.

EDUCATION

The adult literacy rate in Botswana is 83 percent, which is roughly the same percentage of Batswana children who attend primary school. In secondary school the numbers drop off, with 61 percent enrollment for boys and 67 percent enrollment for girls. Fewer boys attend secondary school because they drop out and find a job to boost their families' incomes.

At the University of Botswana, the only national university in the country, students can earn degrees in business, education, engineering and technology, humanities, science, social studies, and graduate studies. In 2001 the university built a new library, which is the largest public library in southern Africa. Private

Traditional circular huts are still built in rural Botswana. Traditionally, the walls are made of mud and cattle dung, while the roofs are thatched. The large house at the back of this village is where the chief lives.

institutions such as Damelin of South Africa and NIIT of India have opened schools in Botswana to teach business and computer skills. Some college-age students prefer to study in England or Europe.

HEALTH CARE

The biggest threat to the Batswana is the spread of HIV (human immunodeficiency virus). This virus causes AIDS (acquired immunodeficiency syndrome), an illness that is almost always fatal if left untreated. AIDS destroys a person's immune system, making him or her fatally susceptible to normally non-threatening diseases. Botswana has the second-highest HIV/AIDS infection rate in Africa, with nearly 25 percent of its adult citizens infected.

The government has been trying for years to educate the people of Botswana about how to prevent AIDS. In 1995 the U.S. Centers for Disease Control, in conjunction with the Botswana Ministry of Health, initiated the BOTUSA Project to inform the public about the spread of tuberculosis and

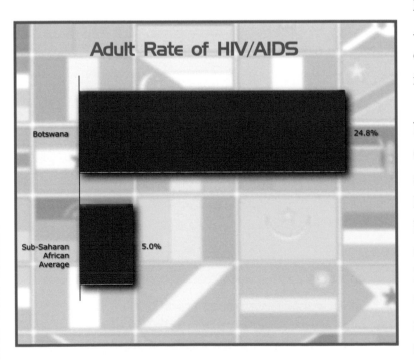

Adult Rate of HIV/AIDS

Botswana 24.8%

Sub-Saharan African Average 5.0%

AIDS. Other programs have included messages on billboards, posters, leaflets, and bumper stickers. Former President Mogae made a point of addressing the issue in nearly every speech he gave, emphasizing the risks in blunt, tough language. He even took an AIDS test himself and revealed the results, which were negative. Current President Ian Khama has continued this no-nonsense policy by stressing the connection between alcohol and unsafe sex. His decision to place a heavy tax on all alcoholic beverages is at least partly an attempt to curb such practices and reduce the overall rate of new infections.

On January 1, 2004, a new law went into effect that made HIV tests mandatory for all patients who visit government hospitals or clinics, except if patients specifically decline them. This has made it easier for the Batswana to overcome the stigma of the disease and find the courage to face their test results.

Botswana is one of 15 countries receiving funding from the United States through PEPFAR, the President's Emergency Plan for AIDS Relief. American businessman Bill Gates is personally funding much of the government's AIDS campaign and was instrumental in bringing in the international drug company Merck to help those who are already HIV positive. Merck has pledged $50 million dollars to fight AIDS in Botswana, and the company sustains the lives of 35,000 Batswana by supplying them with unlimited access to their anti-retroviral drugs.

Unfortunately, despite the best efforts of the government and private charities, HIV continues to spread in Botswana. Seventy-five people die of AIDS in Botswana every day, and every five hours another person is infected with HIV. More than 95,000 children have been left without parents because of the disease, and the government has to find a way to take care of them. Life expectancy for the Batswana has dropped from 65 years to 38 years. President Khama and other leaders in the government know that if the country is to survive, much less thrive, conquering AIDS is a challenge that must be met.

ARTS

Botswana's artistic tradition, which began with the rock paintings of the Tsodilo Hills centuries ago, is alive and well in both the cities and the rural areas. The handmade baskets created by the women of Botswana are some of the most beautiful in all of Africa, and traditional potters continue to mold their wares from the clay of local rivers, just as their ancestors did. Woodcutters craft elaborate sculptures, furniture, and bowls. Tapestry artists spin, dye, and weave wool, producing colorful rugs and wall hangings. The Botswana National Museum in Gaborone shows both contemporary and traditional works of art.

Music is also very important to the Batswana. Traveling through the cities, one hears music everywhere: in the shops and restaurants, on the street corners, and in the taxis. Children are taught dancing and singing from the time they are very young, both in their family life and in their primary schools. Traditional, percussion-based music is still the most popular, but many people are also in church choirs that feature more Western-style melodies.

Culturally speaking, the high point of the year in Botswana may be the

Dzalobana Bosele Arts Festival, a youth-led, alcohol-free celebration of music, theater, and poetry. Though only a few years old, it is already a massive countrywide program that encompasses all the major cities and towns in Botswana. Adults and children alike are encouraged to share their talents.

SPORTS

Say the word "sports" in Botswana and most people will think of one thing: football (the sport Americans call soccer). The British introduced football to Botswana during the protectorate era. The Botswana Football Association regulates professional football teams, such as Gaborone United and Township Rollers, and many children, especially in urban areas, grow up playing the game. For most people in Botswana, playing or watching football is a way to relax. However, there have been instances of fans taking things too far and starting fights and riots.

Though the Batswana love their football, it is not the only sport they play. Interest in chess is at an all-time high since female player Tuduetso Sabure took the trophy for Botswana at the African Chess Championships in Lusaka, Zambia, in 2005. She also earned the title of Woman International Master, a lifetime title that is Botswana's highest honor in the sport.

Botswana has many growing cities. (Opposite) Gaborone is home to the University of Botswana, which boasts the largest public library in southern Africa. (Right) An Air Botswana turbo-prop plane sits on the tarmac at the airport in Maun.

6 Botswana's Growing Cities

ALTHOUGH MANY PEOPLE IN BOTSWANA still live in rural areas, its cities grow larger every year. Lured by the promise of plentiful jobs and modern living accommodations, the Batswana are increasingly happy to exchange their traditional ways for a sophisticated city lifestyle. With business and industry making healthy strides, the urban areas of Botswana will no doubt continue to thrive as centers of both economic and cultural life.

GABORONE

Gaborone, the capital of Botswana, was founded in 1890 by its namesake, Chief Gaborone Matlapin, near the southeastern border with South Africa. It replaced Mafeking as the capital at the dawn of independence in 1965. With a population of about 200,000 people, Gaborone is the largest city in the country. Its small airport handles international flights, and it is located on the country's major railway line. Gaborone is also the home of the University of Botswana, which was founded in 1971.

The construction business in Gaborone is booming, with new offices, hotels, and shopping malls springing up to service both residents and tourists. Visitors to the city are often struck by how clean and neat the city is. The streets, which have names like Hippopotamus Street and Zebra Drive, are well-maintained, with accurate, helpful traffic signs and cement gutters. Though it might seem small by international standards, Gaborone is a thoroughly modern city, and its restaurants, nightclubs, and casinos are some of the finest in Africa. Gaborone is a center of the diamond industry; it is also close to asbestos and manganese mines, which provide jobs for many of its citizens.

FRANCISTOWN

The site of Africa's first gold rush, Francistown still holds many reminders of its past, such as the remnants of abandoned mines. It is the traditional home of the second-largest ethnic group in Botswana, the Bakalanga. Francistown's reputation as a center for industry and commerce grows every year. About 85,000 people live there, making it the second-largest city in Botswana.

Called the "Capital of the North" by the Batswana, Francistown is actually on the country's eastern border with Zimbabwe. Many Zimbabweans are drawn over the border to buy imported goods in its well-stocked stores. The main attraction for European and American tourists is Francistown's proximity to the Makgadikgadi Pans and its flocks of pink flamingos. Several fine hotels and many shops and restaurants cater to these tourists and provide jobs for the local people.

The main road in Francistown, Blue Jacket Street, was named after the clothing of Sam Anderson, one of those early prospectors who put the city on the map.

SELEBI-PHIKWE

A town of about 50,000 in northeastern Botswana, Selebi-Phikwe's most important industry by far is mining. Bamangwato Concessions Ltd. (BCL) is the largest mining company in town, excavating copper and nickel ore and employing workers from all over Botswana. BCL has the longest cable-belt system in the southern hemisphere. The workers' jobs are physically exhausting and at times even dangerous. Day after day they mine the ore, which is then transported for smelting. The mines of Selebi-Phikwe have been in operation since 1973, long enough so that several generations of some families have worked in them.

In addition to the mines, Selebi-Phikwe is home to textile plants and other manufacturing facilitites. Selebi-Phikwe also offers its residents shopping malls, libraries, parks, sports facilities, and a golf course. Its airport, which accommodates international flights, is being upgraded. Though tourists sometimes pass through Selebi-Phikwe on their way to other places in Botswana, few stop there because there are no nearby tourist attractions.

MAUN

Maun, located in the heart of northern Botswana, has become "safari central"—a vital part of this country's growing and thriving tourist industry. Its proximity to the Makgadikgadi Game Reserve, Nxai Pan National Park, Moremi Game Reserve, and Chobe National Park makes it the perfect home base from which to embark on all sorts of wild adventures. Banks, auto mechanics, and modern supermarkets make life easier and more pleasant for both tourists and the 45,000 year-round residents.

A tailor in Maun converses with a customer.

Another factor in Maun's modernization is the government, which designated Maun the administrative center for the northern and western areas of Botswana. Office buildings were built and roads were paved to service the arrival of government workers and their cars. Even the traditional mud huts that are still built in the surrounding suburbs have a touch of the modern— tin soft drink cans are often used as insulation.

A small airport and several shuttle bus companies service the tourism industry in Maun, and there are hotels, lodges, and guesthouses for those planning to spend more than one day in the city.

LOBATSE

Nestled in the hills of southeastern Botswana, Lobatse, named after a chief named Molebatse, is a busy town of about 30,000. Lobatse was the first city in all of Botswana to have a tarred road, which was laid specifically for a visit from King George VI and his family in 1948. The king, his wife Queen Elizabeth, and their daughters Elizabeth (the current queen of England) and Margaret arrived by rail on a white train. Greeted by 25,000 people, the royal family was entertained by a brass band and mounted troops on parade. The king inspected the soldiers and presented medals, but when it was time for tea, two separate parties were held—one for whites and one for blacks.

Today, things are very different in Lobatse. Modern and integrated, it is the home of the High Court of Botswana and the headquarters of the Department of Geological Surveys. The Botswana Meat Commission, which regulates the production and trade of one of the country's most important exports, is also located in Lobatse.

A CALENDAR OF BOTSWANA'S FESTIVALS

January

The Batswana ring in the new year with the Western world on January 1, **New Year's Day**.

March

The **Maitisong Festival** in Gaborone is a celebration of music, theater, and dance that uses both indoor and outdoor performing spaces. The modern performances at this festival are famous for their uniqueness and creativity.

April

Christian Botswanans celebrate **Good Friday**, **Holy Saturday**, and **Easter**. They also celebrate **Easter Monday**, which is usually a day of more secular traditions, such as egg hunts.

May

As is done in many countries, May 1 is **Labor Day** in Botswana. People take the day off work and rally in support of workers' rights.

July

Sir Seretse Khama Day, observed on July 1, honors one of Botswana's greatest leaders.

August

The **Kuru Traditional Dance and Music Festival** helps keep traditional dance styles and percussion-based music alive in Botswana.

September

September 27 is **International Tourism Day**, a holiday to celebrate the vital service industry.

Botswana Day is observed on September 30. This is a day for all patriotic Batswana to show their love for their country.

December

The **Dzalobana Bosele Arts Festival** is organized by the youth of Botswana but provides entertainment to people of all ages. It is a countrywide festival with exhibits and shows in every major city and town.

A CALENDAR OF BOTSWANA'S FESTIVALS

On **Human Rights Day**, December 10, the peace- and freedom-loving Batswana celebrate the rights of the individual in a democracy.

For the 20 percent of people in Botswana who practice Christianity, December 25, **Christmas Day**, is a holy day. For all other Batswana, it is a relaxing day off from work. Like their former British rulers, the Batswana also celebrate **Boxing Day**, the day after Christmas on which additional presents are given.

RECIPES

Vegetable Potjie

5-6 medium potatoes
1 medium butternut squash
5 large carrots
2 ears of corn
1 small turnip or rutabaga
1 stalk celery
1/2 cup oil
2-3 onions
4-6 cloves garlic
1 tsp. salt
black pepper to taste
2 tsp. dried oregano
2 tsp. dried basil
1 cup vegetable stock

Directions:

1. Wash the vegetables and cut into chunks. Heat the potjie (cast-iron pot) over medium heat until a little bit warm, then add oil.
2. When oil is hot, lightly cook onions and garlic. Arrange vegetables in layers on top of onion and garlic mixture.
3. Add potatoes, then carrots, then corn, then squash, then turnip, and finally celery. Sprinkle on the seasonings and herbs. Pour stock over the final layer.
4. Cover the pot with its lid and simmer over medium-high heat for 1-1/2 to 2 hours. Leave the lid on until the cooking time is finished.

Bobotie

1 cup milk
2 slices bread
2 onions
1 clove chopped garlic
1 tbs. curry powder
1 lb. ground beef
4 tbs. strawberry jam or marmalade
1 oz. slivered almonds
1 tsp. salt
2 eggs
4 bay leaves

Directions:

1. Pour half of the milk over the bread and let it soak. Sauté the onion and garlic in oil.
2. Mash the bread and add to it the onion and garlic, spices, meat, jam, half of the almonds, and salt. Mix.
3. Transfer to a baking dish. Mix eggs with remaining milk and pour over meat mixture. Sprinkle with almonds, and top with bay leaves.
4. Bake at 350°F for 50 minutes. Top should set and might have to be covered to keep from burning.

Isophu (Bean and Corn Soup)

2 cups lima beans
2 cups fresh corn off the cob
2 tsp. salt
4 cups water

Directions:
1. Bring water to boil, add beans, corn, and salt.
2. Reduce heat and simmer gently for two hours, adding water when necessary.
3. Cook until beans and corn are soft.

Botswana-Style Chicken Casserole

1 whole chicken
4 tbs. oil
4 medium onions, chopped
2 large tomatoes, chopped
salt and pepper to taste
5 tbs. flour

Directions:
1. Cut chicken into pieces. Heat oil and fry chicken pieces until golden brown. Add onions and cook for five minutes.
2. Add tomatoes and seasoning, simmering gently for 45 minutes or until cooked through. Thicken casserole with flour mixed with a bit of cold water.

Fried Mopane Worms

4 1/2 lbs. dried mopane worms
1 tsp. salt
3 tbs. cooking oil
1 onion
1 tomato, peeled and cut in small pieces
1 Tbs. peri-peri sauce

Directions:
1. Soak the dried mopane worms in warm salt water till swollen. Drain.
2. Boil the worms in water and drain again.
3. Fry the worms in oil in a saucepan. Add the onion, tomato and peri-peri sauce and simmer till the tomato is cooked.

GLOSSARY

AIDS—an acronym that stands for acquired immunodeficiency syndrome. This disease, caused by the human immunodeficiency virus (or HIV), destroys a victim's immune system, leaving it unable to defend the body against illnesses. Although AIDS can be treated to prevent the most debilitating symptoms, there is no cure for the disease.

agriculturalist—a person who farms to produce most or all of his or her food.

apartheid—a discriminatory political system in South Africa in which blacks and people of mixed race were segregated from white citizens. Whites also received more rights and privileges than did blacks.

barter system—a system of trade in which one person offers goods or services, rather than money, in exchange for other goods or services.

carat—a unit of mass used to measure diamonds and other precious stones, equal to 200 milligrams.

Cold War—a worldwide struggle for political, military, and economic dominance involving the United States and the Soviet Union between 1946 and 1991. The superpowers avoided traditional armed warfare by supporting different sides in smaller regional conflicts outside their own countries.

dialect—a regional variety of a language, with differences in vocabulary, grammar, and pronounciation.

ecotourism—a form of tourism in which care is taken to cause as little damage to the land or local ecology as possible.

expatriate—a person who has left his or her homeland to live in another country, but does not become a citizen of that country.

gross domestic product (GDP)—the total value of goods and services produced in a country annually.

guerrilla fighters—a group of people who use unconventional military tactics, such as ambushes, raids, and sabotage, to harass and defeat a larger, less mobile, enemy. Guerrilla tactics are often used by insurgents who wish to overthrow a government.

hydration—keeping enough fluids in one's body.

migrants—animals (particularly birds) that travel from place to place with the seasons in order to breed or to avoid unsuitable weather conditions.

miombo—semi-evergreen trees that grow in semi-arid regions.

monopoly—a situation in which one company controls an industry or is the only provider of a product or service.

protectorate—a country or territory that is defended and controlled by a more powerful state.

transfrontier conservation—a practice in which two or more countries agree to work together across their borders to protect a large environmental region.

wildcat strike—a sudden strike that is not authorized by the workers' labor union.

PROJECT AND REPORT IDEAS

Reports

Write one-page biographies on any of the following people:

- Seretse Khama
- Pete Le Roux
- David Livingstone
- Ketumile Joni Masire
- Festus Mogae
- Laurens van der Post
- Ian Khama

Presentations

Make a mural on cardboard of the industries for which Botswana is most well known. Paste magazine clippings of diamonds, beef, and tourism on the cardboard. Write two or three paragraphs about each industry and present it to your class.

Choose five animals that live in the Kalahari Desert. Find a large photo of each one and write a short essay to accompany each photo. Tell your class about the history of each animal and its status today. Is it endangered? What does it eat? Does it live in the Kalahari year round, or is it a migrant?

Plant Poster

Botswana is home to many beautiful plant species. Choose one to draw in colored pencil on a poster board. Next to the plant write a description of where it can be found in Botswana, how it is used by the people of Botswana, and any unique or unusual characteristics.

Flag of Botswana/Discussion

Paint the flag of Botswana on a large piece of paper (you will need black, white, and sky blue paint). After the flag is completed, hang it at the front of the class and discuss the events leading up to Botswana's independence and the success of democracy in Botswana. Why has democracy worked in Botswana when it has not worked in other African counties? What can those countries learn from Botswana?

CHRONOLOGY

First millennium B.C.:	Khoesan disperse throughout southern Africa, including the area that is now Botswana.
ca. 200 B.C.:	The Khoesan split into two different tribes, the Khoe and San.
A.D. **300:**	The Bantu migrate into Botswana.
1600:	The first Dutch explorers visit the region of modern Botswana.
Early 1800s:	The Tswana migrate north into Bostwana.
1867:	Mining begins with the arrival of the first European gold prospectors.
1885:	The British establish a protectorate called Bechuanaland after being asked to defend the country from the Boers.
1890:	The British protectorate is extended to the Chobe River.
1951:	Seretse Khama is deposed and exiled by the British.
1952:	Rioters protest Seretse Khama's exile.
1959:	Copper mines are established.
1960:	Bechuanaland People's Party (BPP) is established. Britain approves new constitution for Bechuanaland. Executive Council, Legislative Council and African Council are established.
1961:	Seretse Khama appointed to Executive Council. Khama founds the Botswana Democratic Party (BDP).
1965:	Gaborone becomes the capital of Botswana. The BDP wins the first legislative elections and Seretse Khama is elected prime minister.
1966:	Bechuanaland is granted independence and becomes the Republic of Botswana.
1967:	Diamonds are discovered at Orapa.
1969:	The BDP wins the general election. Seretse Khama is reelected for another term.
1977:	The Botswana Defence Force is established.
1979:	The BDP wins the general election; Seretse Khama is reelected again.
1980:	President Seretse Khama dies. Vice president Ketumile Joni Masire becomes president.
1984:	In the general election BDP wins a majority and Masire is reelected as president.

1989:	The BDP again wins a majority in the general election. The National Assembly reelects Masire as president.
1991:	Twelve thousand public sector workers are fired after a strike in which they ask for increased wages.
1994:	In legislative elections the BDP secures 53 percent of the vote. Masire is reelected by the National Assembly.
1997:	Botswana's constitution is amended. The president is limited to two five-year terms, and the voting age is lowered from 21 to 18.
1998:	Masire resigns as president and retires. The vice president, Festus Mogae, becomes president. The Botswana Congress Party is established after a split in the BNF, and is declared the official opposition to the BDP.
1999:	A six-day state of emergency is declared to resolve a voter registration problem. Festus Mogae is confirmed as president in the general election.
2000:	President Mogae says AIDS drugs will be made available free of charge from 2001.
2002:	Kalahari San take the government of Botswana to court to challenge a forced eviction from their land. The case is dismissed on a technicality.
2004:	Hundreds of workers are fired after a strike at Botswana's largest diamond-mining company.
2004:	President Mogae secures a second term in a landslide election victory.
2006:	Kalahari San win four-year legal battle to hold on to their ancestral lands.
2007:	The beef industry is threatened by foot and mouth disease.
2008:	Festus Mogae steps down as president on April 1, turning over the presidency to Ian Khama, the son of former president Seretse Khama.
2009:	Botswana cuts diamond production in an effort to boost demand. Ruling BDP party wins elections and President Ian Khama retains the presidency
2010:	Higher diamond prices usher in an economic recovery; AIDS epidemic continues.
2011:	U.S. First Lady Michelle Obama visits Botswana in June.
2012:	In March, the governments of Angola, Botswana, Namibia, Zambia, and Zimbabwe agree to form the Kavango Zambezi Transfrontier Conservation Area.

Good, Kenneth. *Diamonds, Dispossession & Democracy in Botswana*. Oxford: James Currey, 2008.

Kras, Sara Louise. *Botswana* (Enchantment of the World. Second Series). Danbury, Conn.: Children's Press, 2007.

Levert, Suzanne. *Botswana* (Cultures of the World). Salt Lake City: Benchmark Books, 2007.

Scott, Robyn. *Twenty Chickens for a Saddle: The Story of an African Childhood*. New York, Penguin, 2009.

Wheeler, Patti and Hernstreet, Keith. *Travels with Gannon and Wyatt: Botswana*. Snowmass, Colo.: Claim Stake Publishing, 2010.

Travel Information

http://travel.state.gov/travel/cis_pa_tw/cis/cis_1071.html
http://www.lonelyplanet.com/botswana
http://www.travelnotes.org/Africa/botswana.htm

History and Geography

http://africanhistory.about.com/od/botswana/Botswana.htm
http://www.africa.com/botswana
http://kids.yahoo.com/reference/encyclopedia/entry?id=Botswana

Economic and Political Information

http://www.gov.bw/
http://news.bbc.co.uk/2/hi/africa/country_profiles/1068674.stm
http://botswana.usembassy.gov/

Culture and Festivals

http://www.2camels.com/maitisong-festival.php
http://www.everyculture.com/Bo-Co/Botswana.html

Embassy of the Republic of Botswana
1531-1533 New Hampshire Avenue, NW
Washington D.C., 20036
Tel: (202) 244-4990
Fax: (202) 244-4164
Website:
http://www.botswanaembassy.org

U.S. Department of State
Bureau of Consular Affairs
2100 Pennsylvania Ave. NW, 4th Floor
Washington, DC 20037
Tel: (202) 736 9130

U.S. Embassy in Botswana
P.O. Box 90
Gaborone, Botswana
Tel: (+267) 395-3982 / (+267) 395-7111
Fax: (+267) 318-0232
Email: ConsularGaborone@state.gov
Website: http://botswana.
usembassy.gov/

Tourism Authority
Fairgrounds Office Park
Block B, Ground Floor
Plot 50676
Gaborone, Botswana
Tel: (+267) 391-3111
Fax: (+267) 395-9220
Email: board@botswanatourism.co.bw
Website: http://www.botswana
tourism.co.bw/

INDEX

78

Numbers in ***bold italic*** refer to captions.

CONTRIBUTORS/PICTURE CREDITS

Professor Robert I. Rotberg is Director of the Program on Intrastate Conflict and Conflict Resolution at the Kennedy School, Harvard University, and President of the World Peace Foundation. He is the author of a number of books and articles on Africa, including *A Political History of Tropical Africa* and *Ending Autocracy, Enabling Democracy: The Tribulations of Southern Africa.*

Kelly Wittmann has written two other children's books, *The European Rediscovery of America* and *Explorers of the American West.* She lives in Chicago.